I0558065

COUNSELING WORKBOOK FOR KIDS 9-12

30+ Fun Activities to Build Confidence, Overcome Anxiety and ADHD Disorders through CBT Exercises and Coping Strategies to Self Regulate Daily Life

By

Carol D.

Prime Pen Publisher

© Copyright 2023 by Prime Pen Publisher - All rights reserved.

Without the prior written permission of the Publisher, no part of this publication may be stored in a retrieval system, replicated, or transferred in any form or medium, digital, scanning, recording, printing, mechanical, or otherwise, except as permitted under 1976 United States Copyright Act, section 107 or 108. Permission concerns should be directed to the Publisher's permission department.

Legal Notice

This book is copyright protected. It is only to be used for personal purposes. Without the author's or Publisher's permission, you cannot paraphrase, quote, copy, distribute, sell, or change any part of the information in this book.

Disclaimer Notice

This book is written and published independently. Please keep in mind that the material in this publication is solely for educational and entertaining purposes. All efforts have provided authentic, up-to-date, trustworthy, and comprehensive information. There are no express or implied assurances. The purpose of this book's material is to assist readers in having a better understanding of the subject matter. The activities, information, and exercises are provided solely for self-help information. This book is not intended to replace expert psychologists, legal, financial, or other guidance. If you require counseling, please get in touch with a qualified professional.

By reading this text, the reader accepts that the author will not be held liable for any damages, indirectly or directly, experienced due to the information included herein, particularly, but not limited to, omissions, errors, or inaccuracies. You are accountable for your decisions, actions, and consequences as a reader.

About The Author

As a writer of numerous successful and widely published books on topics of mental and physical health in children, Carol has effectively used her professional skills as a family therapist and freelancing sports and physical education to write not only her professional experiences and knowledge but also practical experiences from her personal life as a woman in different social obligations; wife, mother and daughter.

Much of her publications are about child psychology and kids' mental health. She has written many books for families that have kids with impaired mental health as a means to provide family therapy to those who cannot access traditional means of therapy and are desperate so that they can heal and nurture their kids to lead a better family life.

CONTENTS

MY DEAR PARENTS

To my readers, the parents whose kids are suffering from mental problems like ADHD and other anxiety issues. I cannot stress enough with words how much difficult it is to see your child go through such a challenging phase of life. It is one of those times we find fault in ourselves, our parenting, our lifestyle, our choices and our decisions from the past and present.

As parents, we are instinctively drawn towards the commitment of protecting and nurturing our kids from birth till the day they become independent. We come to terms with bitter realities, hard truths, many life-altering realizations and various choices in our parenting journey that all lead to one single purpose; a positive outcome for our child. Most of the time, we hope and are sure that it plays out well and the situation goes smoothly, while other times, our actions or decisions backfire, causing more damage than repair and maybe, on the unluckiest of days, even damage an already good thing going on. But worry not.

There is something else of great importance that my mature readers must know: You still have a chance. The fact that you are reading this book means you want to help your child overcome the burdens of deviated mental health. You still have a chance at salvaging something. Unlike those unfortunate parents, who have been too late, unable to find the necessary means to help their child, who may have also lost the battle to save their families, you still have your child to look after and cure their problems. Being humble and grateful is a gift blessed to a few. I believe that the parents reading this book are some of those few. So please take a chance to reconsider your emotional and familial gains and losses before delving deeper into this book.

It goes without saying that when one family member is affected, the whole family is affected. The entire system gets shaken. So, in most cases, it is not just the affected child that is to be looked after, but also other loved ones in your home, your spouse, your other children, an elderly grandparent and yes, even your companion animals (pets). They (your pets) may not be able to speak, but they feel equally. It takes courage, patience, determination and an iron will to overcome such difficult times and walk out victorious. The journey is not easy, but anything is possible with great focus, will, and a positive attitude.

No parent wishes to see their child in a dismal state. But you must "Hold On" and work your way into liberty with your family and especially your affected kid. I am sure this book will guide you every step of the way, not just in therapeutic activities and exercises but also your general knowledge regarding anxiety and ADHD and their cure through CBT. I wish you the best in life, the best for your child and best of luck reading!

FOR MY YOUNG READERS

Do you feel overwhelmed at certain points in life? Does anxiety, negative thinking and overthinking overwhelm you on a regular basis?

If you are reading this book alone, I can tell you that you are already strong in so many ways! I welcome you to this book and its contents. Read as much as you like, there are some things you will understand, but many others will fly over your head (you would not be able to understand). So, kindly give this book to your parents/guardians as it is addressed directly to them. They will better understand it and instruct you how to use this accordingly. But wait! Before you go, do you want to hear a secret?

The first secret is that I know your potential. There are so many good things to come in your life; the great accomplishments you will gain. Yes, I know your strengths and weaknesses. I know you will be a great person as time moves on.

If someone like me can realize who you are as a person, then so can you, my dear reader. You are still young for most concepts in this book. But rest assured, this book is mainly to help you be calm and relaxed by instructing and educating your parents to give you a good amount of fun, exciting, engaging activities to take care of your emotions and mental state.

Stress, anxiety, negative emotions and thinking are also part of your life but do not dive deep into them or let yourself be controlled by them to a great extent. Your life is ultimately in your control, kids. Choose the right options, explore goodness, prefer positivity and above all, never lose faith and hope in yourself.

LET US BEGIN

If I say that the human brain is predictable and easy to understand, it would be a downright lie. Understanding someone else's nature or personality is no small task. The entire principle of human nature can be credited to a person's psychology. Same goes for humans of all ages, especially children.

Before starting this book, it is vital for parents to understand what it means for children to have poor mental health, its dangers, treatments and how it affects their lives into adulthood. From a conservative point of view, some people may think, what depression or anxiety could a child possibly have? Kids are too young to feel the pressures of life yet? They do not have jobs, life and independency to have stress of all that.

It is a simple concept, just as positivity and goodness do not discriminate and can affect anybody at any given time, same goes for negativity. It can affect anyone of any age at any given time or place. The main point here to keep in mind is that we are talking about stress, anxiety and depression that forces children to undergo ADHD and other anxiety issues. Their ability to be calm, to self-regulate, do healthy emotional processing is heavily impaired which can have serious negative effects that become permanent into adulthood if left unattended.

A lot of kids get gloomy and hopeless and worry about things all the time. Intense apprehensions can show themselves at various ages. Regardless of whether they are in a safe and caring environment, separation anxiety can cause severe discomfort in young children. While it's normal for kids to feel some apprehension and worry at times, anxiety and melancholy can cause such feelings to continue or even worsen. These conditions are sometimes referred to as "internalizing disorders" due to the fact that they manifest largely in a person's internal experiences.

BEFORE YOU READ MY (NOVELETTE)

This is a short yet well-detailed account of my past personal experience dealing with child depression and anxiety. As a mother of five, three teenagers and two twin kids, my job as a mom has been strenuous enough. One of my twins, Jacob, suddenly started to develop erratic behavior in his daily life. Initially, I merely thought of it as typical day-to-day stress from school and academic work and tried supporting and helping him accordingly, but as time went on, his behavior started to solidify and become severe.

He slowly started to show signs of depression and anxiety, after which my husband and I became very worried. Since he was very anti-social then, there was no direct way of safely communicating with him to track the underlying cause. Also, at the time, my family was going through the burden of the financial crisis, and unfortunately, because of that, we could not afford clinical therapy for him. In such times, it was also stressful and painful for us that our kid was affected, and we could not help him. This emotional state was heavy for us as parents because all of our other children had never gone through such a phase in life. This was new to us, and of course, it was difficult to navigate new experiences.

After a few days of trying to help him at home by ourselves by whatever means necessary and how much knowledge we had regarding a kid's deviated mental health, our efforts did not bear many results.

Then I came across a board-certified psychologist who was a freelancer and, before that, worked at an NGO for troubled kids. He offered to help with some waived fee. It was enough for us to manage, and without thinking twice, we quickly started his therapy. To my surprise, I found his treatment method quite unorthodox at first, even doubting his capability as a clinician. Almost within a month, my kid started getting better, more open, social and physically regaining his strength. That psychologist would mostly just give him worksheets and exercises and various in-house activities to do at home or his clinical office. He also prescribed short-duration medications, but mostly his focus was on cognitive therapy. In the beginning, my son hesitated to do any of these activities, but we encouraged and participated in these activities to engage him in them. Thank God, all of it worked, and my child is all better and living his life happily now.

All these incidents inspired me to help other such children in need, I was not a board-certified psychiatrist or psychologist working directly in the medical field at the time, but I vowed to learn and get into this career as well. I applied for diplomas and post-degree short courses in subjects that focused on family therapy. I passed them with great scores but did not go into practice right away. I picked up small freelancing or private jobs and patients as my diplomas were then board-certified. For about two years, I learned and gained experience, and now I am a well-established family therapist and writer.

I am sincerely optimistic that my book will help you guide your children into a stronger mental health that leads to a resilient and happy lifestyle so that they can become successful adults and stay joyous in their lives.

CHAPTER 1: STUDYING THE KIDDO BRAIN

For this chapter, parents must be mentally and emotionally prepared to learn about ADHD and, depression & anxiety in general. This chapter will discuss the details and important information regarding ADHD and its consequences in affected children. This chapter is of utmost importance so please read this carefully. After all, how can you remedy a problem if you have no fundamental knowledge regarding it.

1.1 ADHD

When it comes to childhood neurodevelopmental diseases, Attention Deficit Hyperactivity Disorder (ADHD) ranks high. In most cases, it is first identified in childhood and continues until maturity. Children with attention deficit hyperactivity disorder (ADHD) sometimes struggle with focusing on one task at a time, avoiding distractions, and regulating their activity levels.

Symptoms and Indicators

All kids struggle with attention and behavior issues at some point in their lives. Children with ADHD, however, do not outgrow their symptoms. The symptoms persist, vary in intensity, and can disrupt one's life at work, home, and with friends.

Possible symptoms in a child with attention deficit hyperactivity disorder include:

• They tend to daydream quite a bit.

• Lose or neglect something. Many of them wriggle or fidget, talk too much, make blunders or take risks that they don't need to.

- Find it difficult to say no to things and awkward to switch roles.

- Experience a difficult time getting along with others.

Depending on which symptoms are most prominent, ADHD can manifest in one of three ways:

Predominantly Inattentive Form: The person has difficulty getting things done, staying focused on the task at hand, or paying attention in social situations. The individual has trouble focusing or remembering basic tasks.

Hyperactive-Impulsive Manner: Lots of fidgeting and rapid speech. Maintaining inactivity for any length of time is challenging (e.g., for a meal or while doing homework). Younger kids, especially, may constantly be on the move. The person has problems controlling their impulses and often feels agitated. Someone who is impulsive might speak before they think it through, take things from other people, or interrupt them frequently. The individual has difficulty waiting their turn or paying attention to instructions. A person who is more prone to acting on impulses than others may be at increased risk of harm.

Both of the aforementioned symptom groups are present in the person to an equal degree; this is known as a Conjugated Form.

You must keep in mind that the presentation may evolve over time with the symptoms.

What Triggers ADHD in Kids?

Researchers are looking at the root causes and potential risk factors for ADHD in an effort to develop more effective treatments and preventative measures. Current research reveals that heredity plays a major part in ADHD, but the exact cause(s) and risk factors for the disorder are still unknown. Current research has connected ADHD to genetic predisposition.

Scientists are looking into potential risk factors and causes that are not tied to genetics.

- Brain damage

- Prenatal or early life exposure to environmental hazards (such as lead)

- The dangers of alcohol and cigarette use during pregnancy

- Premature birth

- Underweight babies

The widely held beliefs that too much sugar in the diet, too much television, parenting, or social and environmental variables like poverty or family upheaval promote ADHD are unfounded, according to research. In some cases, these and other factors may exacerbate symptoms. The data, however, is not sufficient to infer that these are the major causes of ADHD.

Effects

Anxiety, depression, lack of self-regulation can affect a child as a result of ADHD.

I.2 Anxiety & Depression in Kids

» Anxiety

Anxiety disorders are diagnosed when a kid either fails to outgrow the normal concerns and worries of childhood or when those worries become excessive and prevent the child from focusing on their academics, family life, or recreational pursuits. Anxiety disorders come in a wide variety, some of which are:

- Have extreme anxiety while separated from parents (separation anxiety)

- Phobias involve an abnormally high level of apprehensions about a particular object, activity or instance, such as animals, insects, or medical appointments (phobias)

- Having a severe fear of going to school or other places with lots of people (social anxiety)

- Anxiety and concern over potential negative outcomes (general anxiety)

- Repeatedly suffering from attacks of extreme dread accompanied by symptoms including a racing heart, shortness of breath, and/or a feeling of lightheadedness, nausea, and/or sweating (panic disorder)

Anxiety can manifest in children as concern or fear, but it can also cause them to act out in anger. Some people with anxiety also experience bodily symptoms, such as exhaustion, headaches, or stomachaches, and others have difficulties sleeping. Some children with anxiety choose to keep their concerns to themselves, making it difficult to recognize their symptoms.

» Depression

There are times in every child's life when they feel sad or hopeless. Still, some young people experience sadness or loss of interest in activities they once enjoyed or a sense of helplessness or hopelessness in the face of circumstances over which they have no control. Depression in children is diagnosed when there is an ongoing feeling of melancholy and loss of hope.

Common symptoms of depression in youngsters include

- Being consistently down, depressed, or irritable

- Irreverence toward or disinterest in engaging in pleasurable activities

- Displaying irregular eating habits, such as eating significantly more or less than normal

- Displays irregular sleep habits, such as much more or less sleep than usual

- Experiencing shifts in energy, such as chronic fatigue, lethargy, or agitation.

- Having trouble focusing

- A sense of helplessness, uselessness, or shame

- Behaving in a self-destructive way, including self-harm

A child's suicidal ideation or actual suicide plan can be triggered by severe depression. When looking at the causes of death for young people (10-24), suicide ranks high.

Some kids may not express their despair or show signs of sadness, but that doesn't mean they aren't struggling. Another symptom of depression in children is acting out or not caring about things that would normally motivate them, which can lead to their peers misidentifying them as troublemakers or lazy.

CHAPTER 2: UNDERSTANDING THE ROOTS

Before moving to the advanced sections of the book, you must know the basics of why, when, how or where counseling is done for your kid. This chapter will discuss in detail what therapy and counseling are used for child mental health, what parents must know about the social and psychological development of kids in early age and the importance and benefits of therapy and counseling in young kids dealing with depression and anxiety. The topics discussed are delivered from a general perspective.

2.1 Introducing Therapy & Counseling

A common definition of therapy describes it as the process of curing or improving the symptoms of a disease or disorder. The common conception of therapy is that it can only be done by medical experts or primarily by medical professionals at a clinic or hospital, and this is partially correct. It is very important for you to be aware that there are many various styles and approaches to treatment. This book will focus on self-therapy as a treatment for mental health issues.

What exactly is "self-therapy"? It refers to the practice of rewarding oneself. This can be accomplished not only via medication but also through the completion of particular errands, activities, or workouts that will assist your child in relieving stress and regaining energy and strength and regulating their mental health. In a broad sense, activities that promote relaxation and approaches that integrate the mind and body might be categorized as forms of self-therapy.

All that is required from you is to dedicate some time and effort to your kid, as well as to fully commit to what you are doing and maintain consistency. I assure you that your and your kid's efforts will not be in vain.

The second core aspect for parents to learn is about counseling. The word counseling hails from the ancient Latin word 'consilium,' which converted to 'counseil' in Old French and counsel in modern English. Irrespective of its linguistic history, the main meaning of the word is still the same. The word counsel means advice or consultation.

The concept of advice and consultation is as old as humanity itself. We see the stories of many historical figures implementing this concept in their works and lives. Most people today, due to social or cultural differences or improper context, mistake consultation as an intervention. Counseling is much of a learning input and output resource. Think of counseling your kid as giving them life lessons or important life skills that are beneficial for their health and existence. Counseling can be verbal, like discussions, talks and non-verbal i.e., through activities and exercises like in this book.

2.2 Interacting & Connecting with Your Kid

Now that you know about the concepts of therapy and counseling, the next step is to understand bonding with your kid. Being social is an inevitable nature of humans, and kids being kids, are in their prime years of gaining and receiving social inputs.

As parents, it is vital for you to understand that your kid is going through a challenging phase in life, and they need your support and you to be around to help them. The activities in this book can only help you if you interact and connect with your children first. The first step is interaction, and the second step is connection. Socializing with your kid, asking them, listening to them and providing them with chances are some of many ways of interaction. An effective and successful interaction leads to a strong and solid connection.

1. Show Interest & Compassion

Establishing a connection with your kid can be completed in a fairly short amount of time. The people you care about will appreciate even the smallest efforts you make to show them you care.

- For instance, when your child is talking to you, put down what you're doing for a moment, look them in the eye, and listen carefully for the next five minutes.

- Tell your child on a regular basis that you love them, and be sure to remind them of this frequently.

- Tell them why you are proud of them and why they make you proud.

Small things like this go a long way in showing that you care about the other person and that they are your first concern.

2. Teach, NOT Punish

Instead of scolding or correcting your child for their error, use it as an opportunity to teach them something.

Negative contact cannot teach youngsters how to behave positively, and it harms the relationship that exists between a parent and child. Inappropriate forms of discipline, such as physical abuse, pose a threat to the growth and development of children.

- There are more methods available besides just punishing a youngster for bad behavior.

- It is considerably more successful to teach with kindness, and it develops a deep relationship with the learner.

Because you are able to connect with the students while you are teaching, this method of discipline is the most effective.

3. Be Silly

It has been demonstrated that laughing together makes relationships stronger.

- Accept the humor that is already there in your life and laugh alongside them.

- Make a joke, make a funny noise, perform a ridiculous dance, sing a made-up song, roughhouse with each other, and anything else that comes to mind.

4. Embrace Negative Emotions

When we were sad as children, we were frequently reassured that "it's ok," "it's no big deal," and "it'll go away."

Do you think that they actually helped us feel better? I bet not.

Simply put, it led us to believe that our thoughts and feelings were either incorrect or irrelevant.

It is only normal for parents to desire to relieve their children of those terrible feelings as quickly as possible. Yet ignoring their emotions won't solve the problem.

If your child is experiencing anger, ignoring their feelings can only make the situation worse.

- One of the quickest ways to develop a connection with your child and calm them down when they are unhappy, angry, or sad is to be attentive to their feelings and empathize with them.

- Name their intense emotions and validate their feelings as a way to demonstrate that you comprehend how they are currently feeling.

- Try to avoid saying anything that could possibly invalidate them, either directly or indirectly.

- Demonstrate to them that you are concerned about how they are feeling.

Respond as per the following examples:

- "It is very troubling. If I were treated in that manner, it would make me angry too."

- "It seems really unjust; don't you think? I completely understand why you feel so strongly about this matter."

Instead of trying to stifle their feelings of anger and frustration, it's better for children to learn to understand and work through such feelings.

2.3 Realizing Early Development of Children

The foundations of mental health are also set during this formative period; as early events affect the structure of the developing brain. When this process is interrupted, it can have long-lasting effects on a child's ability to learn and interact socially. Many of society's most expensive problems, such as incarceration, homelessness, and dropout, are preventable if we invest in children's early social and educational contexts.

Mental Health Problems Affect All Ages

Little children are not immune to serious mental health issues. Characteristics of mental health issues like anxiety, ADHD, ADD (Attention Deficit Disorder), CD (Conduct Disorder), BD (Bipolar Disorder), and PTSD (Post-Traumatic Stress Disorder) can be seen in young children, while neurological problems like autism can manifest themselves as early as infancy. However, when compared to adults and older children, young children have quite distinct ways of reacting to and making sense of emotional experiences and traumatic events. As a result, making a diagnosis in a young child might be far more challenging than in an adult.

• Genetic Factors

The effects from experiences or from environment on the genes are what controls their expression.

The mental health of children is influenced by both genetics and environmental factors. Genes are not deterministic. The chemical "signature" of our surroundings can either approve or block the instructions contained in our genes, which inform our bodies how to function. An unstable mental health foundation can be set early in life by the interaction of genetic predispositions and prolonged, stressful experiences.

• Exposure to Toxic Stress

It has been shown to alter brain structure and increase susceptibility to the development of long-term mental health issues. Toxic stress can have long-lasting negative consequences on physical and mental health, as well as on a person's ability to learn and perform academically, because of its impact on the developing brain and other organ systems. Family stressors, such as prolonged financial insecurity, have been linked to increased vulnerability to mental illness. Children under the age of five are more susceptible to the negative effects of parental mental health issues, substance misuse, and domestic violence.

While it is never too late to start, doing so sooner is ideal. There are limits to a child's ability to emotionally heal from adversity, yet some people show exceptional capacities to overcome the extreme challenges of early, persistent mistreatment, trauma, and emotional injury.

Removing a child from a traumatic environment and placing them with a loving family can have a positive effect on their development, but this is not always the case. Children who have gone through trauma often have trouble with self-regulation, emotional adaptability, relationships, and self-understanding, even after they have been in a safe environment for some time. When children triumph against adversity, it is usually due to the unwavering dedication of caring adults. These results highlight the need for proactive measures to protect young children from situations that pose substantial psychological risks.

2.4 Significance of Therapy & Counseling

Children's mental health is intrinsically linked to the health of their parents and families. Abuse, threats, chronic neglect, and other forms of psychological injury in these relationships are strong predictors of later mental health issues in children. Nonetheless, the positive impacts of connections can operate as a buffer, protecting young children from the harmful consequences of other stressors if they are consistently responsive and helpful. In order to alleviate the strains placed on children, it is necessary to first address the strains experienced by their families.

- During counseling, your kids can talk to an objective third party who will listen without passing judgment and affirm their feelings.

- Counselling increases your kid's sense of self-worth and motivates them to draw the conclusion that their own wants and needs are significant and deserving of acceptance.

- After a kid experiences the first fruit of their parents' counseling efforts, they are more likely to keep opening up and working through their difficulties.

- One good deed might inspire a chain of positive deeds and reactions.

- Avoidance and procrastination are common human responses, but they can be uncovered and addressed with the help of counseling your kid.

- Counselling helps your kid become more cognizant of and take responsibility for their future negative behavior.

- Counselling offers helpful strategies for recognizing and overcoming destructive thought patterns that cause one to form unfavorable opinions of oneself and others.

- Counselling facilitates the development of an awareness of and ability to challenge a kid's own self-talk.

- Counselling promotes more nuanced and accurate inferences about oneself.

- Counselling allows one to make more accurate comparisons to oneself rather than to others.

- It gives kids who are living in unusual or challenging conditions access to information and resources that would otherwise be unavailable to them, allowing them to better understand the bigger picture and gain insight into the significance of particular occurrences and patterns.

- It helps kids view difficult situations more objectively and constructively.

Good therapy and counseling involve not letting your kid avoid or ignore painful emotions. You, as parents, must know that it is often in the midst of suffering that the greatest opportunity for growth and change can be found. In most cases, this is the key to finally solving problems that friends and family have avoided addressing.

CBT therapy in itself is a counseling method, therefore, you can help your kid battle anxiety and depression, counter their ADHD by giving coping strategies and exercise and activities which will help them self-regulate their lives.

CHAPTER 3: COUNSELING & KIDS: A PERSPECTIVE

If you are to perform a test in a science lab, you readily go through the detailed information on how to do it, such as procedure, the materials required and potential prediction of results. Same is the case with counseling and therapy in order to have effective and result-yielding counseling and cognitive therapy for your kid. This chapter discusses the fundamental rules or factors regarding approaching kids, having patience with them, what things to tell, and what it means to engage them in exercises and activities that develop positive mental health in them.

3.1 Approaching Kids

The first step in any situation in life is how you approach people and situations. Parents need to know that they cannot approach kids regarding any subject as they would do with other adults. Children are too young and naïve to understand advanced concepts and higher levels of context, which is why, whether in speeches or activities, parents must always use simplistic ways of providing knowledge and opportunities to kids.

Giving too much information to kids all at once or talking to them at an advanced or higher level that is beyond their understanding can cause more harm than good. Parents should not hesitate to be a little childish and rekindle their inner child to interact with their kids. By doing so, they connect with their children in a stronger and more efficient way, giving rise to better flow of communication. Such an approach will enable your kid to feel more open and secure. Then you can talk to them regarding their mental health.

3.2 Patience with Kids

If you apply values that are considered virtuous in your counseling skills, then without a doubt, helping your kid in their mental health will be efficient, effective and will bring positive results. It is not easy interacting and connecting with kids facing mental health problems, as it seriously affects their typical moods and causes them to have unpredictable behavior.

Either way, whatever the situation may be, the responsibility of maintaining our calm falls on us as parents. It is a lot easier to tell your kid off or scold them to solve the situation. That is never the answer or the right way to correct their problem. In fact, what feels easy for you can actually end up hurting them emotionally or mentally and put them on the path of more severe negative mental health.

So, please, be patient with your kids. There are times when they need love and care the most, so make sure to keep your calm and cool and have a lot of patience with them. Even though they may annoy you or put you in a place of anger sometimes, they still are kids. They are still learning and growing up to be teenagers.

3.3 Information to Give to Kids

After establishing a strong bridge of interaction, connection and communication along with positive values with your kid, the next step is to know how much, what kind of, in what way, through which medium or in what context you should give information to your affected kid.

It is common knowledge for all parents that they cannot give kids most advanced level of information as it is. Such information ought to be diluted and made more concise to be able to relay to them. Young children have a more limited capacity for understanding; thus, they require less knowledge and fewer details than older children do. Little children in preschool pay the most attention to items that they can see. For instance, they may have inquiries regarding a certain individual who possesses an odd physical feature or who is acting in an unusual manner. Those who are sobbing and clearly disturbed, as well as others who are shouting and angry, would likewise be brought to their attention very quickly.

The needs, worries, information, and experiences your child has had with mental diseases should be in your knowledge. When discussing mental health conditions, parents should consider the following:

- Direct your communication toward the intended recipient only (which is your kid)

- Communicate on a level that is suitable for the age and phase of development of the child you are talking to.

- Dialogue should take place at a time when the youngster is feeling secure and at ease.

- Parents should monitor their child's reactions throughout the conversation.

- Parents should either back up or slow down if the child appears confused or upset.

3.4 Engaging Kids in Brain Exercises

In order to engage your kid in exercises and activities listed in this book, you must first make sure to activate their interest and motivation from the root. This involves analyzing their work and play both at school and home and coming with effective strategies while reviewing the previous results of interaction/connection, approaching, and patience in mind. The following list is given as a general concept through three examples for kids dealing with ADHD, depression and anxiety. Identify why, when and where your kids lack engagement and motivation and act accordingly.

If the child has trouble sitting still and listening when they are in a circle or a small group, they may not be on the same cognitive or linguistic level as the other children.

Engagement Can Be Done By:

Provide the child with some sort of object to hold.

Ensure that the youngster has a good view of the instructor, the book, or the materials.

- Provide the child with a copy of the materials that the instructor is using.

- Ensure that the youngster is properly supported and that they are comfortable in the seat.

- Provide the child with a visual agenda of the activities that will be carried out while they are with the group.

- Encourage and compliment the youngster more frequently when they are sitting by providing them with positive comments.

- Place an adult or another child who has agreed to assist the child in sitting with the group next to the youngster in question.

If the kid does not focus on an activity and wanders Engage Them By:

- Provide the youngster with a limited selection of places and activities to pick from.

- Provide the child with a limited selection of resources to choose from when participating in activities.

- You should set a timer for the youngster and then give the child specific instructions to hold and play until the timer goes off.

- Ask other children around your kid who are of the same age to ask about suitable games and exercises and which one to choose.

- Go over a "play plan" with the child one-on-one, and then lead them to the appropriate place so they can get started.

- You should give the youngster visual guidance on the activity they are participating in. For instance, when it comes to painting, you could provide the child with a prototype and then instruct them to "create one just like this." When it comes to blocks, you could provide the child with a picture of straightforward block construction and instruct them to "make this out of blocks."

- Create a unique container and fill it with toys that you are sure the child will like playing with. When you are unable to provide the child with a redirection to help them become engaged in the activity, present the box.

- You should organize activities that will give the child a chance to get away from their friends or the noise for a while (as the level of activity in the classroom can sometimes become overpowering). A story on tape that the child may listen to with headphones, a reading tent where the child can hide away, a nice area with pillows, or a peaceful space with toys that is limited to only one child are some examples of these types of activities.

- You should provide the child their own personalized, visual timetable so that they can better comprehend the events of the day and choose which activities they would like to participate in.

- Check to see if you have allotted a sufficient amount of time to play. Because there is not enough time allotted for children to play in a concentrated manner, some children may wander because they want to participate in all of the activities.

- You and the other adult in the activity should take turns monitoring the child's actions and assisting them in locating and beginning to participate in an activity.

If the child puts up a strong front in avoiding encounters with other children and adults.

They Can Be Engaged By:

- Modify your expectations. Make a mental note of how long the child will remain engaged before starting to resist. Modify your expectations for the child's level of engagement by working at only doubling that time (for example, if the youngster is only able to stay focused for three minutes at this point, work toward six).

- Take into account the child's preferences and employ those particular toys and activities to encourage interaction with and tolerance of a play partner (adult or child).

- To facilitate the child's participation in parallel play with a peer, you should first establish a center that is reflective of the child's interests and then give two of each of the resources included in that center.

- Take into account the child's level of skill in play, and then select activities that are suitable for that level. For instance, if the youngster seems to excel at dumping and filling, provide them with activities along those lines. Provide opportunities for the youngster in each of these areas so that they can participate in the activities.

- Seek playmates who will ask the child to join them in their games or follow the child's lead and play in a manner that is parallel to what the youngster is doing.

CHAPTER 4: ROLE OF CBT TO SELF-REGULATE & CALM YOUR KIDS

This chapter will tell you all that you need to know about CBT and how it affects kids. Do not confuse CBT with mental illness as it is actually the name of a therapy. This chapter also highlights and explains various activities used in CBT to calm your kid and self-regulate their lives so they can push past ADHD and anxiety and boost their mental health.

4.1 Cognitive Behavioral Therapy (CBT)

As a form of psychotherapy, CBT combines cognitive therapy with behavior therapy to help affected people identify and alter unhelpful ways of thinking, feeling, and behaving in favor of more constructive ways of thinking, feeling, and behaving.

During CBT treatment, irrational ideas are identified, debunked, and replaced with rational ones. It helps patients focus on the here and now while also being time-sensitive, so they can achieve their most pressing life goals. Cognitive theory, on which CBT is founded, posits that one's reaction to a given situation is determined more by one's own interpretation of that scenario than by the situation itself.

Fundamentals of Cognitive Behavioral Therapy

The goal of cognitive-behavioral therapy (CBT) is to help patients alter their way of thinking, their way of perceiving the world, and their actions as a result. The concept that feelings, thoughts, and actions are all intertwined is fundamental to cognitive behavioral therapy. That is to say, the way you are feeling and thinking about something may affect the choices you make. When you're under a lot of pressure, whether at home or in the classroom, it might distort your perspective and cause you to behave in ways that are out of personality for you. The idea that these patterns of thought and action are malleable is central to cognitive behavioral therapy as well.

The following are some of the areas that CBT can help youngsters master:

- Negative mental processes

- Impulsivity

- Disobedience

- Irritabilities

Rather than unfavorable responses, try:

- Enhanced sense of one's own worth

- Enhanced self-control, problem-solving abilities, and a wider toolkit of coping techniques

After making CBT methods second nature, they will remain useful for the rest of your kids' life.

The founder of cognitive behavioral therapy (CBT) identified three levels of thought:

- Core Values

- Negative or Bad Preconceptions/Predictions

- Instinctively Negative Ideas or Pessimistic Thinking

Core Values

The things you learn and experience as a child will significantly impact your worldview as an adult. They provide the basis for your fundamentally pessimistic outlook on life and its people and things.

Bad Predictions

Focusing on the negative can lead to false conclusions, but that is not how we operate most of the time. This leads to a distorted view of the world and an inaccurate understanding of data. In this context, "mental distortion" refers to skewed thinking methods exacerbated by unpleasant emotions and ideas.

Uncontrollable, Pessimistic Thinking

Involuntary, persistently bad perceptions of reality are called automatic negative thoughts (ANTs). Because of their fleeting nature and ability to provoke negative emotions, they might be difficult to detect. You can fight against pessimistic thoughts by reframing them more rationally and effectively.

Role of CBT:

- It is used as a therapy in ADHD sufferers.

- It is used to treat people with anxiety and depression due to ADHD

- It helps affected people to build a strong sense of self-regulation their lives.

- It provides affected individuals with coping strategies.

The main or intended chapter of the book includes diverse, easy, engaging and enriching activities and exercises for your affected kid. All activities in this book are for kids who are suffering from anxiety or depression as a result of ADHD or any other reason.

4.2 CBT Activities

This part will help your youngster with anxiety or depression gain practical, immediate tools for life improvement through CBT therapy.

Behold, awesome activities and exercises!

Schedule your Negative Thinking

It may seem counterproductive to set out time in your day just for negative thoughts; however, if you do this in a normal, disciplined manner, you can move on from your damaging feelings rather than wallow in them. Maintain a notebook in which you write down your pessimistic thoughts, and give yourself ten to fifteen minutes daily to sit with the feelings these thoughts bring up.

Though changing negative thoughts is easier said than done, it is a habit that needs repetition and effort to become successful. You must train yourself to identify the beginnings of destructive thinking processes, interrupt them, and retrain your mind to focus on constructive or uplifting ideas.

Situation	Negative Perceptions	Sensations in the body and mind
Provide some background on what caused your gloomy outlook.	What was going through your head at the time?	Describe the emotions you experienced. How intense was that sensation.

Keep a Journal

You should write down your negative ideas in a notebook or another written record. Write down the notion, then explain why you had that thought in the second step. If you want to efficiently organize and assess your thoughts and feelings, typing things down enables you to do it in a more effective manner than simply ringing them in your mind.

Negative Thought	Reason For Having It	Positive Thought
"They'll probably expel me soon. I can never do anything right. As far as I know, this is it. Obviously, I'm not cut out for this institution."	I had an error in class, for instance.	"Of course, I made a blunder, but hey, that's okay. I will, as I usually do, find a method to overcome this challenge."

Have Faith in The Immediate Positive Future

This modest yet useful phrase could support you in restoring perspective. It can occasionally seem as though an unwanted thought will never leave your mind. Nonetheless, thoughts are never permanent and are always passing through one's mind. Discovering a mantra that helps you reduce the impact of undesired ideas, such as "This too will pass" or "My ideas are fleeting," could be beneficial.

Currently I'm distressed because _____

_____

_____

That distressful situation occurred because _____

_____

_____

I am hopeful because _____

_____

_____

I have faith that this will get better when _____

_____

_____

I am positive regarding my future because _____

_____

_____

Express A Notion in a Different Way

Our minds are incredibly talented when it comes to generating narratives that we see as being based on reality. So, if an unwelcome idea is allowed to persist within your head, it can acquire an unhealthy amount of power over time. Consider putting the notion down or even simply expressing it loudly to see if that influences how it impacts you.

Examining Different Points of View

Choose three viewpoint characters from a tale you just read and explain what it was like for them. Finally, evaluate your viewpoint against that of each character. Provide concrete instances to back up your answers.

Character:

Narrate from the point of view of the protagonist.

_____

_____

You:

To what extent do you share my viewpoint, and how do yours differ?

_____

_____

Character:

Focus on the viewpoint of the character you're describing.

_____

_____

You:

Please explain how your viewpoint differs from the norm.

_____

_____

Character:

Tell it from the point of view of the character.

_____

_____

You:

So, what makes your take on things unique?

_____

_____

Character:

Explain how the character feels.

_____

_____

You:

What about your viewpoint? Is it the same or different?

_____

_____

Black n' Red Card Exercise

Playing this game will encourage you to communicate your emotions and thoughts through cards.

To begin, take the card that is currently on top of the deck of cards. In case you get a red card, you get 1 point. In the event that you receive a black card, you must respond to one of the questions listed below in descending order from 1 to 6. When you provide an answer to the question, you will receive 2 points. You will be awarded three points if you choose a jack, queen, or king! At the conclusion of the game, you can exchange your points for the following prizes: 1–10 points = 1 prize; 11 or more points = 2 prizes.

- What are some activities that you love participating in?

- Share two things that brighten your day and make you joyful.

- Name three main things you worry about often.

- When you are anxious, what sorts of things do you repeat to yourself in your head?

- Name two physical changes that take place in your body whenever you are anxious.

- When you are anxious, what helps you feel better and more in control?

Converting Negative Thoughts

Since certain thoughts are based on fact, it's possible that limiting those thoughts won't always be effective. Instead, it might be better to work on developing a sense of acceptance in particular situations. This entails not making any efforts to change or eliminate the concept or event but rather accepting it in its current state as it is and working towards its conversion into a positive outlook and healing from the negative.

Negative Thoughts	Conversion Results

Check Your Feelings

As the goal of CBT is to help children (and adults) understand the relationship between their thoughts and actions, a feelings thermometer is a great option to consider when planning cognitive behavioral therapy exercises for children. Using this exercise, you and the child can check that they have a firm grasp on the fundamental emotions, and then talk about how we can feel multiple versions of each sensation.

Creating a "Feelings Thermometer" with a child is an excellent way to teach them to recognize their emotions, see the links between their ideas, feelings, and actions, and ultimately learn to manage their own emotions.

Feelings Mercury Reading		
Angry	**5**	Shouting
	4	
	3	
	2	
Easy	**1**	Resting
Present Emotions	**0**	Present Actions

Fire Breathing Activity

Some children with ADHD have more frequent episodes of anger than other children. Anger and irritation are additional symptoms of ADHD in adults. Although widespread, these feelings have a negative impact on interpersonal connections, conduct, and domestic harmony.

Those with ADHD, both children and adults, often feel their emotions more strongly than their non-ADHD friends. Inability to control one's emotions or maintain them within a healthy range is what's known as "emotional dysregulation."

The worksheet below is part of a game concept called mad dragon. This helps kids with breathe their fiery anger out like a fierce dragon whilst also helping them deal with it too.

When you look at me, what expression do you have on your face?

_____

_____

What are some of the things you say?

_____

_____

How do you carry yourself when you're in an upset mood?

_____

_____

When you feel angry, what changes take place in your body?

_____

_____

Other methods for dealing with my rage

_____

_____

What do you hope to accomplish by channeling your anger?

_____

_____

Have you made any progress in understanding your anger?

_____

_____

What makes it easier to deal with your anger?

_____

_____

Affirming Positivity

An affirmation is a phrase that encourages you to change a negative thought or belief about yourself. They aid you in confronting and conquering any destructive ideas.

If you reiterate the affirmations often enough and give them some credence, you will see good results. The more you use positive affirmations, the less often you'll give in to those destructive thoughts.

It has been found that practicing positive affirmations for ADHD can be quite helpful for children who suffer with poor self-esteem or a lack of confidence. Having a positive outlook and higher levels of self-esteem are two benefits that can be gained through using these techniques.

The use of self-affirming statements is an effective way to assist children develop a growth mindset, self-confidence, and self-belief. Children need constant reassurance of their unique value and strength.

I have what it takes to pass this problem
I am confident and strong
I have faith in myself

Visual Acknowledgement & Gratitude

It may be difficult for your child, who may be feeling melancholy or gloomy, to notice that there are positive parts to life when they are in such a state. Recognizing the positive can be accomplished in baby steps by employing straightforward strategies like this one, which involves recalling the enjoyable aspects of one's day. Even when you are feeling depressed, the process of writing down the nice things that have happened to you will help form new connections in your brain, which will make it simpler for you to focus on the bright side of things.

All that is required of you is to keep a journal in which you record the things in your life for which you are grateful or the most uplifting occurrences that occur on any given day. These can be written or drawn, as you feel convenient.

Today I am thankful for

_____

_____

This person has my gratitude since

_____

_____

Draw a sketch of all the good things that happened to you in this past week in the box below

My biggest blessing in life is

_____

4.3 Coping Strategies for Anxiety & Depression

Kids who are unable to deal with their emotions could act out, which sends the message, "I feel out of control, so I'm going to behave out of control" "Young people who aren't taught good coping mechanisms are more likely to develop an unhealthy relationship with food and alcohol.

Kids who rely on avoidance coping strategies, for instance, might rather play a game with their pals than try to figure out the arithmetic problems they don't understand for their homework.

Then, if they don't do well on the task, it will probably worsen their academic situation. Since they haven't learned strategies to deal with their stress and frustration when attempting the work, these kids are likely to fall even more behind their peers.

The coping strategies discussed in this section are specifically for depression and anxiety in kids.

For Anxiety

Label Your Emotions

You may teach your child this ability by letting them know that it is okay for them to feel angry or sad. It is essential to provide them with assistance while they work to figure out how they feel. Encourage them to give language to their emotion(s) by utilizing "I statement," which will help them take ownership of their feelings without criticizing the sentiments of others. Several examples are listed below:

- "I'm mad"

- "I wish I had company"

- "I'm frightened"

- "I'm frustrated"

- "I'm happy"

- "I'm going to try my best to enjoy myself"

Finally, encourage your children to identify coping methods that will calm them down. Asking younger children what strategies, they would use to help solve difficulties is a good activity to do with them. It could be things like spending time alone, playing with a pet, visiting a trusted friend's house, or having a conversation with someone else. Beginning the process by providing an example of an "I statement" and talking about your own methods of dealing with difficult situations can be quite beneficial.

Leap Of Trust

Kids need to learn that good self-care isn't always about figuring things out on their own; there are times when they need to look to others for support. It is always a great plan to have a "team" of people ready to help, whether family members, friends, teachers, or coaches. This "team" should care for your child and be prepared to assist them. Because it can be difficult to ask for assistance, it will be essential for them to hear and witness others around them asking for assistance when they are in need of it. The most crucial thing you can do to help your child as they grow is to demonstrate these abilities for them.

Attempt Something Comedic

One of the most effective methods of overcoming difficult situations is to laugh. Finding comedy in difficult circumstances may not always make the situation more bearable, but it can help alleviate stress and anxiety by providing a fresh perspective on the problem at hand. Even though you may feel the want to reassure your child by assuring them that "all will be great," there are occasions when this simply isn't enough.

It is quite normal for your child not to feel better immediately; nevertheless, if they do not indicate that they are feeling better, you should continue checking in with them. If they are aware that you will be there for them when they are going through the most difficult circumstances, your words of encouragement will help them get through it.

Art & Craft Therapy

Whether your kid prefers to paint with watercolors, color in a coloring book, doodle, sculpt with clay, or make a collage, engaging in creative activities like these can be an effective way for them to deal with stressful situations.

If you find that your child responds positively to this activity, you should stock up on a lot of different art supplies. Your youngster will eventually turn to the materials to cope with the challenging feelings they are experiencing.

Playing Games

When something bad happens at their school, kids would not stop overthinking it. This leads to them dreading the future and doing something to get their mind off their concerns.

Doing something active, such as playing a board game or kicking around a ball outside, can help shift the focus in their brains and provide a new perspective. Then, they will be able to think about other things instead of fixating on all the things that are making them feel horrible.

For Depression

Test Negative Thinking

Children who suffer from depression have a greater propensity to ruminate, which means they tend to keep thinking about the terrible things plaguing their minds, which only amplifies their emotions of sadness.

When we are depressed, our thoughts frequently become exaggerated and distorted, and as a result, they become excessively pessimistic.

Youngsters can break the habit of ruminating if they recognize when they are having overly pessimistic thoughts, challenge those beliefs, and come up with more constructive and grounded solutions.

This method is referred to as cognitive restructuring, and it is an essential component of cognitive-behavioral therapy.

Kids who are in elementary school or older would benefit the most from acquiring this ability. Since it is an abstract concept, children initially face difficulty in performing this activity since it requires them to think about thinking. Confusing, right? Children can learn how to master this concept and practice "talking back" to negative thoughts from you by doing this activity.

• You are able to assist your child in recognizing when he is thinking something that is unrealistically negative and urge him to inquire himself questions such as the following: "Do I have any evidence to back up this claim?" What advice would I give to a close friend who was having these thoughts?" Is there not another angle from which to view this situation?" "So, let's say that this rumor turns out to be true; in that case, would it be the end of the world?"

Sleep Hygiene

Kids who frequently alter their natural sleep schedule by staying up longer than usual and finding it difficult to go to sleep. Frequently, these young people have to function at school on a few hours of sleep or choose to sleep during the day, missing out on time they could spend with friends.

Depression is typically accompanied by insomnia, so it's not surprising that children who are depressed also have trouble in sleeping. Yet, the difficulty of this condition is compounded by the fact that sleep deprivation makes people more susceptible to anxiety and melancholy, so a poor night's sleep can set off a vicious cycle that ultimately makes gloomy feelings more acute. Also, suppose a child is losing a lot of daylight hours to sleep. In that case, it reduces the chances for them to engage in beneficial activities that can alleviate and prevent depression, such as socializing or participating in sports.

A better night's sleep can be achieved by a combination of practices collectively known as "sleep hygiene" A child's sleep issues may not be entirely resolved by merely adopting these behaviors, especially if she is also experiencing nighttime anxiety, but they are a good place to begin. If you're worried that your child's sleeping habits are contributing to his or her sadness, you should think about the following:

- Put away any electronic devices a half-hour to an hour before night.

- Put down the soda, coffee, or tea 4-6 hours before bedtime.

- If your kid has trouble nodding off, suggest him to read a book or do something else quiet for a while. Instead of tossing and turning in bed, which can make youngsters more agitated and worried, this can help them fall asleep more quickly.

- To assist your child in winding down at night, establish a regular pattern that includes activities like reading aloud and learning relaxation techniques.

It's not healthy to keep waking up at midnight to check the time. If this is the case, make sure your kid can hear the alarm but not see the clock or phone in her room.

- Get your kid moving throughout the day so they can unwind when it's time for bed.

Problem-Solving

A problem can be solved in a variety of ways. Nonetheless, there are instances when children feel helpless and are unable to see the next step forward.

- Sit down with your kid and figure out a solution to whatever issue is bothering them, whether it is how to dress to the dance or how to get back into the habit of doing their chores.

- Write down as many as five different approaches you can think of.

- Then, decide together which one your kid would want to try.

Your kids will naturally improve their problem-solving skills as they age. It is beneficial for kids in the long run if they learn to solve problems effectively now.

Breathing Exercises

Kids can calm their thoughts and bodies with the help of some deep, deliberate breathing. Children can learn to do this by modeling how adults take "bubble breaths."

You may teach children to do this by having them take a deep breath through their nose and then slowly exhale through their mouth as if they were trying to blow a bubble.

You can even train your kids to "smell the pizza" as a different method. Request that they inhale deeply through their noses as if they were smelling pizza. Ask them to blow on the pizza to cool it off. Children can feel better after doing this several times.

Listing Pros & Cons

To assist children in deciding between two options, such as the flute and the violin, have them develop a list of the benefits and drawbacks of each instrument. Assist them in reviewing the list by writing down the benefits and drawbacks of each choice. The ability to see everything laid out in front of them on paper could improve the quality of their decision-making.

When your children are presented with difficult choices, encourage them to write out the benefits and drawbacks of each option. Learning to consider the consequences of their actions is an important life skill, especially when they must make tough moral or practical judgments.

4.4 Worksheet-Based Activities for ADHD

Before we start activities, some important notes on myths vs. facts of ADHD in children.

Myth: All ADHD children exhibit hyperactivity.

Factual Statement: While many children with attention issues are not hyperactive, some children are. Children with this, who are unmotivated and inattentive but not extremely active, may come off as disorganized and disinterested.

Myth: Children with ADHD are never able to focus.

Factual Statement: Kids with ADHD can frequently focus on enjoyable activities. But despite their best efforts, individuals find it difficult to stay focused on monotonous or repetitive tasks.

Myth: If they wanted to, children with this could behave better.

Fact: Despite their best efforts, children with ADHD cannot sit still, remain quiet, or pay attention. Although they may seem disobedient, this does not necessarily indicate that they are doing it deliberately.

Myth: Children with ADHD will eventually outgrow it.

Reality: Do not really wait for your child to outgrow ADHD because it frequently lasts into adulthood. Your child can learn to control and reduce their symptoms with the aid of treatment.

Myth: The best treatment for ADHD is medication.

Actuality: A common treatment for attention deficit disorder is medication. However, for your child, this may not be the best option. Education, behavior therapy, counseling, support at home and at school, exercise, and a healthy diet are all components of an effective ADHD treatment program.

Activities for ADHD (15 Activities)

Asking for Help

Being a youngster has its perks, but it also has its challenges. It's possible that you're having difficulties in your relationships with others, whether it's in terms of friendship, academics, family, or health. Yet, it is always beneficial to share your concerns with someone you trust, irrespective of the nature of your difficulties. Although most children first confide in their parents when they're experiencing difficulties, there are always those who choose to speak with an adult outside the home.

If you're struggling with an issue that you can't handle on your own, reaching out for assistance is your best bet. Simply because you ask for assistance does not guarantee that you will receive it in the form you like. It's not uncommon for the other person to suggest something that's out of your comfort zone or completely unappealing. Not a problem. What you can do is give the advice some thought and see if there's anything you can implement from it. You can seek assistance from someone else, as well. This worksheet below will help your kid embrace the importance of asking for help.

ADHD

Have you ever experienced a major conflict with a member of your family? When you have a major issue, who do you go to for help?

_____

_____

_____

_____

The blackboard was small and difficult to read for Victoria. She hid the fact that she needed glasses because she felt self-conscious about her appearance. She squinted to read what was on the board, but sometimes it wasn't enough. Do you have any words of wisdom for Victoria?

_____

_____

_____

Write down the names of four persons you know who might be able to assist you. Put the reasons beside each name for why you would seek their counsel.

1. _____

2. _____

3. _____

4. _____

Prediction About Events or People

Children with ADHD sometimes can't foresee the results of their behavior. It's possible that you could disregard the consequences of disobeying a rule anyhow, while knowing what's in store if you do. Yet, if you give it some thought, you can anticipate the likely outcomes of most scenarios. It is simpler to maintain self-control if you have developed the ability to anticipate the actions of others and the outcomes of potential situations.

The worksheet below will help your kid use the power of prediction

When you pause to think about it, you can pretty much guess how adults will react to the things you do. Here's a chance for you to try:

_____

Note down three things you could do that would make someone want to hug you.

1. _____ 2. _____ 3. _____

Mark down three things you could do that will get you in trouble or yelled at.

1. _____ 2. _____ 3. _____

List down three things that could help you get good grades.

1. _____ 2. _____ 3. _____

Three things you could do that would make someone say "thank you." Write them down.

1. _____ 2. _____ 3. _____

You Can Handle Medicines

Many children who have ADHD take medication, and the majority of those children report that the medicine is very helpful to them. However, some children experience negative side effects as a result of the medication they take, including difficulty in sleeping, loss of appetite, and even stomachaches and headaches. Even though they do not experience emotions like these, some children are nonetheless anxious about having to take medication. They may be concerned that other children would think that they are unusual, or they may be concerned about the effects that the medication may have on their brain. Always be sure to let your parents know how you are doing and whether or not your medication is causing you to experience any weird side effects or concerns.

Unless you share your feelings, no one can understand them. You can fill in your own experiences with other side effects of ADHD medication. Please indicate how often you agree or disagree with each statement using a scale from 1 to 3 (1 = never, 2 = sometimes, 3 = always). When you're done, take your parents to this chart.

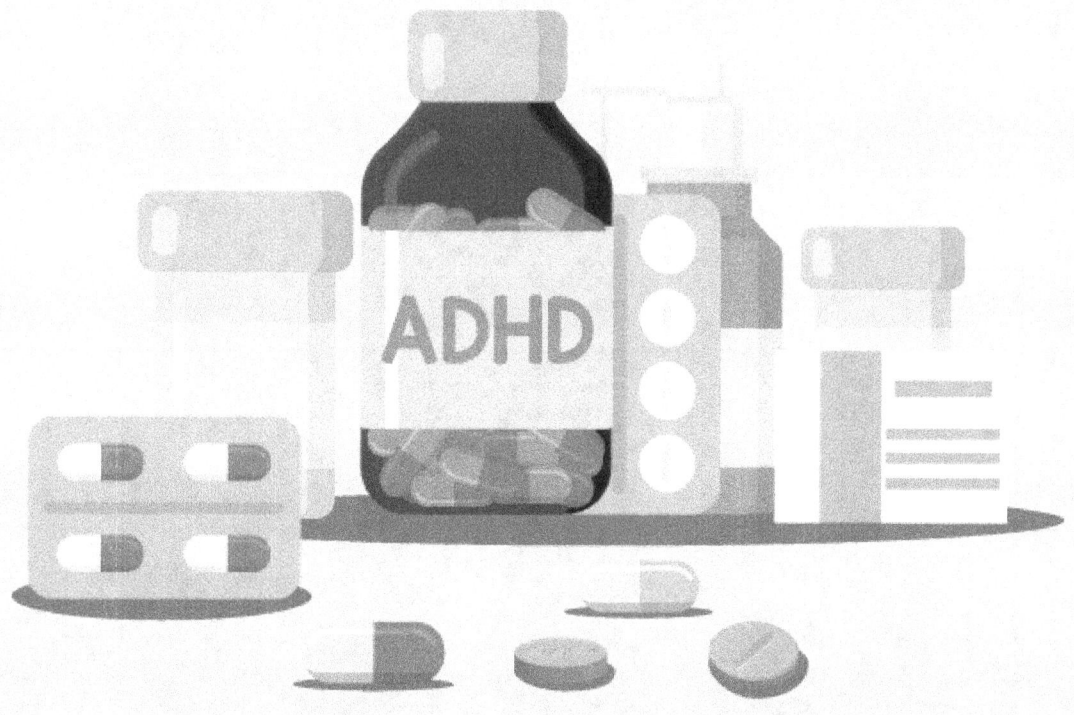

TROUBLE	RATING
My stomach hurts or I get nauseous	
I'm anxious and on edge.	
Whenever nighttime rolls around, I find that I simply cannot go to sleep.	
Dryness in my mouth.	
When I try to poop, nothing comes out (constipation) or they're really loose (diarrhea)	
Sometimes I'll feel lightheaded or have a headache.	
I've been breaking out in itchy rashes.	
My chest is tight and my heart seems to be beating extremely fast.	
Other	

Killing Boredom

One trait shared by the vast majority of children diagnosed with ADHD is an extreme susceptibility to distraction. They are more prone to boredom than their non-ADHD peers. A lot of the time, they have a high IQ but still struggle academically. There's a chance that it's because they consistently fail to accomplish the work required of them in class, whether it's homework, tests, or anything else their teachers have given. But you can train yourself to keep going even when the going gets tough or uninteresting. If an ADHD child is really into a project, he or she can keep at it for hours.

The worksheet below will help you. Try it.

Choose five activities that you enjoy doing and that never seem to bore you.	Now make a list of the top five boring tasks you must complete.
1. _____	1. _____
2. _____	2. _____
3. _____	3. _____
4. _____	4. _____
5. _____	5. _____

Note down what might make each of the uninteresting things you've listed more bearable. Even if you despise making your bed, doing it while listening to your favorite music will help you get through the task more quickly and with less resentment. Even if you don't enjoy doing your schoolwork on your own, having a parent around to chat with can make the time go by more quickly. Try your best to think outside the box and come up with novel approaches to boring chores.

Creating Peace in Your Family

Problems with getting along with one another are normal in families, but the good news is that almost all of these conflicts can be resolved. Members of the family should be given the opportunity to voice their concerns and provide input regarding potential solutions at regular family gatherings.

You may want to advise that your family conducts family meetings if you find that there are regular conflicts and arguments taking place in your home. The effectiveness of family gatherings is typically improved once they are held on a consistent schedule, such as once per week or once every other week. Even if your household is peaceful and everyone is content, holding regular family meetings can help you connect with one another in constructive ways, which will ultimately bring the entire family closer together. When they are well organized, family gatherings typically go more smoothly.

You are welcome to make copies of the worksheet below in order to use it during the family gathering that you are hosting. Before we get started with the meeting, make sure that your parents complete out the page.

When will this meeting begin and end?

Beginning: Concluding:

Who is going to be in charge of the family get-together?

_____

_____

_____

Our topics of discussion will include:

_____

_____

_____

Three important guidelines for the meeting are as follows:

1. _____

2. _____

3. _____

Amusing ways to wrap up a meeting:

_____

_____

_____

Issues settled at the meeting

_____

_____

_____

Avoiding Troubles

Children with ADHD may not stop to consider their actions. Certain regulations and the consequences for breaking them may be forgotten. You can learn to control your emotions and stop doing the things that make grownups upset.

Reflect on the actions you've taken that led to your current predicament. Perhaps you committed an act you now regret because you know it was wrong. Or perhaps you got into problems for something you did, but at the time you didn't consider it to be wrong. You can avoid performing these things by giving some thought to your actions. The guilt and the punishment are unnecessary.

There is a six-point scale you can use to determine the merits of a proposed action. To utilize the scale, simply give your intended action a numerical value. The interpretation of these figures is as follows

1 = People will benefit from this choice

2 = I have nothing to worry about, and I will be content with this choice.

3 = I'll feel okay about making this choice, but it's not the best one.

4 = I'll be happy with the outcome, although it could irritate certain individuals.

5 = Going against established policy.

6 = Illegal action has been taken.

Why I Got Into Troubles	Scale Evaluation

When was the last time you stole something? Why did this occur?

_____

_____

_____

_____

_____

Being Responsible

Growing up involves learning the importance of taking on responsibilities. Children need to learn the importance of taking care of their belongings. Schoolwork must be kept in order and neatly presented, and the students must remember their tasks. The truth is, though, that this is only the beginning. Besides taking care of themselves and their families, children also have responsibilities toward animals, the community, and household chores. It's a lot of work, but the more accountable you are, the more satisfied you'll be with your performance.

Responsibilities	M	T	W	TH	F	S	SU	Total
When no one was looking, I went ahead and finished my assignment.								
Except from the occasional dusting, my room was always spotless.								
I cleaned my room.								
I disengaged and/or unplugged all of my gadgets.								
I managed my wardrobe.								
The food I ate was healthy and nourishing.								

I was responsible pet owner.								
When it came to school, I was always the model student.								
I have never lied to a person.								
I always followed the guidelines to win games.								
My behavior toward adults was always appropriate.								
My arrival at the school was timely.								
After meals, I would assist clean up.								
Without being urged, I completed all of my housework.								

Learning Patience

ADHD kids have a tough time waiting for what they desire. If given the choice between a tiny cookie now and a considerably larger cookie after two hours, they would take the smaller cookie now. You can train yourself to wait for the bigger cookie and reap the rewards of your patience. One of the keys to social success is cultivating a more patient disposition.

"Can't you just sit quietly and remain patient?" is a question you may have heard before. While this is a common criticism leveled at parents of children with ADHD, it's important to remember that their children are not the only ones who have trouble waiting. The ability to exercise patience is a virtue that even grownups sometimes lack. You've probably been stuck in traffic when people are yelling and honking at each other. Or perhaps you've witnessed a grownup becoming frustrated with a slow computer.

The majority of individuals despise waiting, but certain events simply cannot be hurried. These five items should not be rushed.

Growing Up

Your birthday

Seeing the doctor or getting checked out at the hospital

Participating in a sport or picking up an instrument

Developing a Garden

Do you have any further suggestions (at least five)?

1. _____

2. _____

3. _____

4. _____

5. _____

Limiting Digital Time

Most young people enjoy watching television and playing video games. A moderate amount of time spent in these pursuits is OK, but excessive amounts are not recommended. If you spend an excessive amount of time in front of a screen, be it a TV or computer, it can have serious negative effects on your health.

	M	T	W	TH	F	S
Time watching TV						
Time playing video games						
Total Time Spent						

Sleep Management

Kids with ADHD often have trouble falling or staying asleep. Having trouble falling asleep or waking up at odd hours of the night are both possible. If you don't get enough shut-eye, you're more likely to be cranky and distracted during the day.

If you're having trouble unwinding, visualizing a calm, peaceful setting may help. Places worthy of your imagination are listed below. Choose your favorite setting and illustrate it in the box provided. To get the full effect of this, fill in as much detail as possible.

When you're just about to go to bed.

- Pretend you're relaxing on a cloud.

- Let your mind wander while you take a stroll through the forest.

- Just close your eyes and picture yourself relaxing on a beach.

- Let your mind wander to a time when you are relaxing on a boat in the middle of a tranquil, clean sea.

Maintain a set routine before going to bed. Make it a habit to perform the same activity right before going to bed each night.

Fill in your nightly routine in the space provided here.

Listening & Speaking Skills

Children with ADHD often speak their thoughts aloud as soon as they form them, which can be bothersome to those around them. Knowing when to speak and when to listen is a skill that will serve you well in every social situation, from class to casual conversation with friends. As simple as it may sound, strong listening skills need practice. You have to wait for your turn to talk, and then you need to know when to stop speaking. You also have to recognize when it is vital not to speak at all.

When was the last time you got in trouble for raising your hand in class? Why did this occur? Write down below:

_____

_____

_____

Even while it's evident that calling out would get you in trouble at school, the rules outside of school aren't always so black and white. Nobody expects you to put up your hand when you want to chat to your folks or pals, but everyone expects you to speak and listen back and forth. It's kind of riding a seesaw; if no one takes a turn, the whole thing will topple over. If you want to play by the book, consider these guidelines:

- While someone else is talking, don't cut them off.

- Keep in mind the other person's recent words. The following comments ought to be pertinent to that.

- Don't make an effort to prove how smart you are.

- Don't shout or speak too quickly.

- Inquire into the other person's thoughts by asking them questions and then listening to their responses.

- Pay attention to how others react to what you say. (Their nonverbal cues might be more revealing than their actual words.

Diet Management

Some people believe that hyperactivity and lack of focus in children with ADHD may be caused by substances found in common foods. A lot of people think that if you eat right, you can treat your ADHD. Protein, whole grains, vegetables, and fruit, with few or no sweets or processed foods, are generally agreed upon as the cornerstones of a balanced diet.

Few individuals have conviction that you can make a complete shift in your eating habits overnight. The greatest way to make changes to one's diet is gradually, by swapping out a few harmful items for healthier ones at each meal and snack each week. Consider giving it a shot for a month and making one small adjustment each week. You can refer to the accompanying chart as a helpful reminder of just how crucial this is to your health. Rate your progress from week to week using a scale from 0 (no change) to 5 (full change).

	Food To Leave Behind	Food To Replace The One Left Behind	Success Evaluation
Week 1			
Week 2			
Week 3			
Week 4			

Following The Rules

Children with ADHD have trouble in multitasking. Adults often comment on how easily they are distracted by anything. Being easily distracted makes it difficult to focus on a single task, which in turn makes it more challenging to follow directions. Instructions may need to be written down or broken down into more manageable chunks.

Although children with ADHD often have no trouble hearing, they may have trouble recalling what they've been told since they aren't focusing on it. You may get much better at following directions by learning some simple techniques.

Have a look at the paragraphs down here. See if you can decode each sentence and pick up some tips for improving your listening skills. You can find the solutions at the bottom of the page, but they are written upside down. Try first! Don't cheat.

Pay attention to the osnper who is addressing you.

perate instructions to the eltetr.

Get ttnwire instructions by making this request. ckeCh off the steps as you finish them.

In class, record your work using an audio drerocrd.

Keep a botokeno on hand for taking notes at class.

Keep a notebook on hand for taking notes at class.

In class, record your work using an audio recorder.

you finish them.

Get written instructions by making this request. Check off the steps as

Repeat instructions to the letter.

Pay attention to the person who is addressing you.

Recognize Your Talents

Children who with ADHD frequently possess unique abilities. They frequently possess fantastic imaginations, a great deal of excitement, and a variety of incredibly interesting perspectives on the issues at hand.

Do you possess the ability to use your imagination? Try your hand at drawing something unique in each of the two boxes added on this page.

Please illustrate a scene in which you have achieved success.	Make a drawing of an idea for a concept or product that has never been invented before.

List three characteristics that set you apart. If you're struggling to come up with ten, ask your loved ones or educators for their input.

1. _____
2. _____
3. _____

You Can Solve This

The process of maturing and accepting responsibility for oneself includes learning to solve one's own difficulties. Your teachers and parents will appreciate the fact that you are becoming more self-reliant because they will see that you are getting better at solving your own difficulties, which will also make you feel better about yourself. Attempting to solve your particular difficulties does not exclude you from ever seeking assistance from others. If you find that you are unable to handle a problem on your own, it is acceptable for you to seek assistance from a reliable third party.

Consider some of the most daunting challenges you must overcome. Then, pick one of your issues and provide four potential fixes below. Draw a circle around the option that you think is the best. Make a note of your results after attempting it. Explain what you plan to do next if it doesn't work.

Here's My Issue

_____

_____

_____

Resolution 1

_____

_____

_____

Resolution 2

_____

_____

_____

Resolution 3

_____
_____
_____

Resolution 4

_____
_____
_____

So, how did it go when you put your plan into action?

_____
_____
_____
_____
_____
_____
_____

Which additional options will you try?

_____
_____
_____
_____
_____
_____

CONCLUDING THE COUNSELING CASE

In the end, I hope all of my readers have made great use of this book and learned much from it. It is imperative for parents and even general public to understand and accept the importance of child mental health and not disregard this concept because of their own past beliefs or views on life and lifestyle.

Instead, be open and accept the possibility of something adverse at any stage in life but more and equally accepting and open to the chances of solutions and goodness to the said adversity in life. Life is all about balance. Sometimes that balance is thwarted without us noticing or with us finding out very late.

Either way, what matters, is how we push past these hurdles with will and perseverance to regain our life components. Our choices also play an equally important role. With kindness, patience, love, determination, focus and sternness, parents can help their kids who are in dire need of putting their lives back on track.

To all the parents, I wish you the greatest of luck and prayers in strengthening the core aspect of your family!

www.ingramcontent.com/pod-product-compliance
Lightning Source LLC
Chambersburg PA
CBHW081007120626
46546CB00010B/3048